Wonders of
GRAVITY

By Rocco Feravolo

ILLUSTRATED BY
ROBERT BARTRAM

DODD, MEAD & COMPANY
NEW YORK

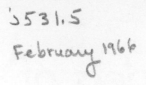
TO MARIETTA, TONY AND LOUIS

CONTENTS

WHAT IS GRAVITY?

G ravity is a force that pulls on things on or near the surface of the earth. Gravity has been pulling on things for millions and millions of years. The early cave man probably had many experiences with gravity without knowing what it was. He found large rocks difficult to lift. Mountain climbing for a long period of time tired him. He certainly felt the effect of gravity if an unfriendly neighbor dropped a rock on his head. An incident such as this may have made him wonder why things fell down instead of up. However, we cannot be sure of what he thought since he did not leave a written record.

Many centuries later Aristotle, a Greek philosopher, believed that all objects fell to the earth because they belonged to the earth. He told the other early-day scientists about this earthly quality that all objects possessed. This earthly quality he talked about was really gravity.

It was not until the sixteenth century that Sir Isaac Newton made some startling discoveries about gravity and gravitation. (Gravitation and gravity are the same thing. "Gravity" refers to the pull on objects near the earth's surface. "Gravitation" is the term used to mean the attraction or pull between bodies in the universe, as between the planets.)

Newton did not make his discoveries by observing the

planets. The story goes that he was sitting under an apple tree when an apple fell to the ground. This made him wonder why things fell down and not up. For some time scientists had known that some force made things fall down to the earth, but it was Newton who first set forth laws about it. All objects, from heavenly bodies down to the smallest particles, have an attraction for each other. This force, or pull, is called gravity, and Newton's ideas about it are called the Law of Universal Gravitation.

Now Isaac Newton did not make up this law the moment the apple hit the ground. It took a long time and deep thought. He first determined that all objects pull on each other. Then he found that the amount of attraction between two objects depended on the mass of the objects and the distance between them. Mass is the amount of matter an object contains. An iron ball has more mass than a rubber ball of the same size. It contains more molecules and they are packed more closely together.

When the rubber and iron balls are thrown into the air they fall to the earth. This is the earth's gravitational attraction on the two balls. The earth has a greater mass than either one of them. It pulls them toward it. Since every object attracts every other object, the earth is also attracted to the two balls. But the amount is so small that it is not noticeable. You cannot see or feel the earth move up to meet them.

Yet the size of an object has nothing to do with its mass or the force of its attraction. If an object as big as the earth had a mass equal only to that of one of the balls, and another object the size of a ball had a mass equal to that of the earth, the larger object would fall toward the smaller one. It is mass that determines the force of attraction, not size.

Newton also stated that the force of attraction depends on the distance between the two objects.

The moon is the earth's natural satellite. It travels around the earth and is about 240,000 miles away from the earth. The earth has greater mass than the moon. If an object was midway between the earth and the moon, it would fall to the earth instead of to the moon because of the greater mass of the earth and its greater gravitational pull.

But if the object was very close to the moon, it would be attracted to the moon. The greater mass of the earth would be too far away to pull the object to the earth.

You would be able to throw a ball a greater distance on the moon than on the earth because the gravitational pull there is much less than the earth's pull of gravity. It would take longer for the ball to fall back to the moon's surface because there would be less force pulling it down.

Gravity is constantly pulling on you and things around you. It pulls on the furniture in your room, keeping it in place. It pulls on your house and school, too. Rocks fall from high places because of gravity. Sometimes many rocks come thundering down mountainsides because of the earth's gravitational pull. Landslides that destroy homes and often kill people are the result of gravity. So are avalanches of snow and ice.

But gravity can bring pleasure, too. It helps you enjoy many sports. Sleigh riding and skiing are winter sports that are possible because of gravity. Can you name summer sports that involve gravity?

It is fun to go downhill on a bicycle. Gravity makes this possible, too. But it is not so much fun to pedal uphill. Gravity pulls down on you and on the bicycle. You must pedal very hard to overcome the pull of gravity and get up the hill.

Water falls because of gravity. When you raise a glass to drink, you are using gravity to get the water into your mouth. Water is falling from a higher to a lower place.

9

Gravity pulls on things everywhere, in high and low places, from the tiny molecule at the very top of the atmosphere to the tiny seashells that rest at the bottom of the sea.

Gravity's pull on objects is in straight lines, pulling them toward the center of the earth. Things that are dropped fall "down" wherever you are in the world. If we could see the people on the other side of the earth, they would appear to be upside down to us.

Houses and automobiles would seem to be upside down, too. "Down" is towards the center of the earth. What appears "up" to us is really "down" to the people living on the other side of the world. Airplanes on the opposite side of the earth would appear to be flying upside down if we could see them.

The early Romans made gravity work for them. Water flows downhill because of gravity. They built large aqueducts that carried water many miles down from the high mountains to the city of Rome. The water flowed through pipes under the streets into the city fountains and into the homes of some of the more wealthy Romans. Today, some cities still get their water in the very same way that the early Romans did.

Long ago water running downhill was used to saw wood and grind grain. The flowing water, usually located near a waterfall,

turned water wheels. The force of the water striking the wooden blades would turn the wheel. The axle of the water wheel was connected to the axle of a circular saw or a grinding shaft. When the water wheel turned, so did the saw or shaft.

Today, large and more complicated "water wheels" called turbines help produce electricity for industry and our homes. Dams are built so that water from a lake flows by gravity through pipes called penstocks. The force of the water spins metal blades in the turbines and they, in turn, spin dynamos, producing electricity.

LAKE   GENERATOR

PENSTOCK

TURBINE

DAM

ACTIVITY

You can make a water wheel with inexpensive materials. You will need: The top of a tin can

           A pencil

           A cardboard circle (2 inches in diameter)

Snip the top of the can as in fig. 1. Now bend each side of the eight sections so they look like fig. 2.

Punch a hole through the center. Insert the pencil through the hole.

FIG. 2

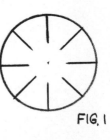

FIG. 1

FIG. 3

Now make a sawtooth edge on the cardboard circle, punch a hole in the center, and attach this "saw" to the pencil as in fig. 3. Hold the water wheel under a running faucet. Make sure the blades of it are struck by the falling water. The wheel and the saw will turn.

The water behind the dams is also used for another purpose. It travels downhill to faraway areas where it is used to water crops. There are many places in this country that were once dry and barren. Thanks to man's ingenuity, and to gravity, these lands have been converted to fertile fields through irrigation.

Maybe you have examined the roots of a plant. Have you noticed how they grow downward, toward the pull of gravity? You can see this happening by doing the following experiment.

ACTIVITY

Plant some bean seeds in a pan or container. Keep them watered. After the bean seeds have grown stems about two inches long, dig several of them up and pin them sideways on a moist blotter like this:

Keep the blotter moist. After several days, you will notice that the stems of the bean plants are pointing up while the roots are pointing down. The tendency for the roots of plants to do this is called *geotropism*. The roots are attracted to the earth.

WEIGHT IS THE MEASURE OF GRAVITY

An iron ball has more mass than a rubber ball of the same size. There are more molecules in the iron ball, even though it is no bigger. If you place the balls on a scale, the iron ball weighs more. Weight is the measure of the pull of gravity. When you stand on a scale to weigh yourself, you are measuring the pull of the earth's gravity on you. The man in the picture here is eating a delicious but heavy meal. If he continues to eat this way he will surely gain weight and increase his mass. The more he weighs, the more earth's gravity is pulling on him.

A person weighing 100 pounds is not attracted to earth as much as a person weighing 120 pounds. The more earth's gravity pulls on you, the more you weigh.

The sun is the largest body in the solar system. It also has the greatest mass and so the sun's gravitational pull is much greater than the earth's. Yet because it is

so far away from the earth, the sun has very little gravitational effect on any objects on our planet. A person who weighs 100 pounds on earth would weigh about 2,800 pounds on the sun. It would be very difficult to lift a pencil on the sun. There would be no way to do your homework. Don't cheer too loudly. The sun's heat would make it impossible for anyone to survive.

The pull of gravity decreases as you move away from the center of the earth. The force of gravity is less on a mountain top than it is in a valley. The passengers in an airplane weigh less in the airplane than they do on the ground.

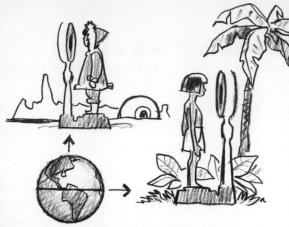

The earth bulges at the equator. The distance from the equator to the center of the earth is greater than the distance from the poles to the center of the earth. You would weigh more at the north or south pole than you would at the equator. A person who weighs 160 pounds at the equator would weigh about 161 pounds at either pole.

GRAVITY METER

Gravity is not the same everywhere on the earth's surface. It is stronger in areas where there is a greater amount of dense rock near the surface. It is less over areas where there is a great quantity of soft soil near the surface. A gravity meter is an instrument that is used to detect differences in the pull of gravity. It is used by oil prospectors to determine the kind of soil.

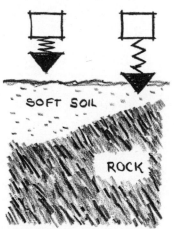

REALLY FAR AWAY

If you weigh 100 pounds on the earth's surface, at a distance of 8,000 miles out from the earth's center you would weigh only 25 pounds. At 40,000 miles from the earth's center, your weight would be a mere $\frac{1}{100}$ of a pound, too light to be really attracted to the earth like a falling apple from a tree.

As you moved away from the earth, the pull of earth's gravity would decrease. There is really no point in the universe where you escape the earth's gravity completely, but at distances beyond 100,000 miles the earth's gravity is very weak.

THE ATMOSPHERE AND GRAVITY

The earth is surrounded by a blanket of air, the atmosphere. The air is attracted to the earth by its gravitational field. We are fortunate to have this ocean of air above us. It shields us from the intense rays of the sun and it contains the oxygen that we breathe. Without air, we would not be able to survive.

The earth's gravity is constantly pulling on the air molecules. Some scientists believe that the atmosphere extends upward as high as 500 miles, but the thickest part of the atmosphere is closest to the earth where the gravitational pull is the greatest. It thins out very fast as the distance from the earth increases.

Air has weight and pressure. We cannot feel the pressure of air because it presses equally in all directions. Sometimes the upward pressure of air helps to overcome gravity.

ACTIVITY

This activity will show you how air pressure can work against gravity. You will need: a drinking glass and a piece of cardboard (4 inches square). Fill the glass with water. Place the piece of cardboard over the glass as shown in the drawing.

Now hold the cardboard and turn the glass upside down. Remove your hand from the cardboard. It stays in place. The weight of the water (the pull of gravity on the water) is not as great a force as the air pressing up on the cardboard. The air pressure at sea level is about 14.7 pounds per square inch. The pull of gravity on the water would have to be equal to about 70 pounds to make the water fall out of the glass.

AIRPLANES AND GRAVITY

Airplanes use air pressure to overcome gravity and stay up in the air. It took man many centuries to learn about air pressure and how to use it to fly through the atmosphere.

Man's interest in flying began when he watched birds fly gracefully through the air. He marveled at the bird's ability to defy earth's gravity. The law of gravitation was not discovered until about 300 years ago, but even before then, man knew that what went up, came down. Man's early attempts to fly certainly had their share of ups and downs.

Sketch of da Vinci's flying machine

Leonardo da Vinci, the great Italian artist, made drawings of flying machines that looked like birds. They had wings that could be made to flap. For many years men tried to fly like birds. Some of them were killed in their attempts to master gravity this way. Then the early pioneers of the air realized that no man had muscles strong enough to flap the man-made wings for a long period of time. Another way had to be discovered to get into the air.

Men began to experiment with balloons filled with hot air to journey skyward. Balloons are buoyant and tend to rise easily anyway.

The idea of using hot air probably came from watching smoke rise out of a chimney. Hot air is thinner and lighter than cold air. Gravity attracts warm air less because it does not weigh as much as cold air.

16

In 1783, a duck, a sheep and a rooster took a balloon ride and were the first living creatures to defy the law of gravity. They rode in a basket attached to the bottom of a balloon that was filled with hot air. As it took them skyward, they must have been surprised. Later the balloon descended to the ground and the farm animals disembarked. There is no record that they got air sick.

ACTIVITY

This activity will prove that hot air is lighter than cold air. For it, you will need:

Cord and masking tape
A thin stick (about 18 inches long)
Two paper bags, the same size

Fasten the closed end of the paper bags to each end of the stick with a short piece of cord and masking tape, so that the open ends are facing down. Tie a piece of cord in the middle of the stick, and balance the stick. Now move the stick so that one bag is directly over a warm radiator. What happens to the bag over the radiator? Does it rise? Explain how this proves that hot air is lighter than cold air.

The early balloonists reasoned that if a balloon could carry animals, a larger balloon could carry human beings. Larger balloons that could lift greater weights were built. The more hot air a balloon could hold, the greater the weight it could lift.

The first air voyage by man took place in 1783, also. Two men traveled in a balloon filled with hot air for a distance of 5½ miles. The flight lasted 25 minutes.

Hot air balloons made it possible to overcome the pull of gravity, but they were often dangerous vehicles. Sometimes the straw fires that were built under the opening of the balloons set the large bags on fire. Professor J. A. C. Charles, a French scientist, experimented with a gas called hydrogen. Since hydrogen molecules are lighter than air molecules, the pull of gravity is less on them.

Professor Charles filled a balloon with hydrogen. He and a friend took a ride in the hydrogen-filled balloon that lasted two hours.

While some men were defying the law of gravity in balloons, others were experimenting with gliders that looked like birds. The balloons filled with hot air or hydrogen rose because they were lighter than air. Gliders are heavier than air and do not rise. To get a glider into the air, the early glider pilot carried his birdlike craft to a hilltop. There he pushed off. Some gliders crashed to the ground below, while others traveled a short distance before gravity pulled them to the ground. Reduced air pressure above the glider wings slows the fall of the glider. Modern gliders, released from the tow lines on airplanes, can ride air currents for long distances.

ACTIVITY

You can prove that a glider falls more slowly than another object of the same weight. You will need two pieces of paper the same size and the same kind (so that they will weigh the same). Roll one piece into a ball. Leave the other one unfolded, like a glider with a wide wing span. Now stand on a chair and drop the paper ball and the plain sheet of paper at the same time. Which one hits the floor first?

Orville and Wilbur Wright owned a bicycle shop in Dayton, Ohio, and in their spare time they built model gliders. They studied many designs and soon became interested in building larger gliders. The first glider they built was flown at Kitty Hawk, North Carolina. In 1903, the bicycle repairmen returned to Kitty Hawk with a different glider. It had a motor on it.

The Wright brothers hoped that the motor would help overcome the pull of gravity and keep the craft in the air.

Orville climbed aboard the strange looking aircraft and flew it a distance of 120 feet, with the motor purring. In 1908, he flew an airplane for one hour, two minutes, 15 seconds at Fort Meyers, Virginia. The airplane was purchased by the United States Army. Aviation was on its way.

The Wright brothers proved that air pressure could be used to defy gravity and keep a heavier-than-air machine in the air.

ACTIVITY

You can show how air can lift an airplane off the ground. Cut a piece of paper two inches wide and eight inches long. Hold the strip of paper against your chin as shown in the drawing.

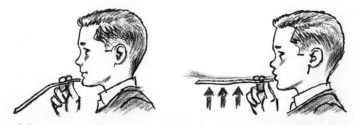

Now blow over the paper. The paper will flutter first. Then it will rise as if by magic. There is no magic involved in this activity. The air moving across the top of the paper reduces the air pressure there. The air pressure under the paper is greater and this causes the paper to rise.

An airplane is lifted in almost the same way. The top of the wings are curved. The air travels faster over the top of the wing. This causes a decrease in air pressure there. The greater air pressure under the wing lifts the airplane off the ground. The faster the air travels over the top of the wing, the more the air pressure there is reduced and the greater the lift.

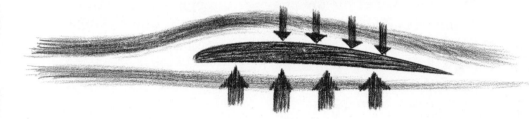

Propellers help to make an airplane move faster. The faster an airplane moves, the greater the lift.

The propeller on an airplane is like the propeller on a boat. A boat's propeller has slanted blades that push the water backward, making the boat move forward.

The propeller blades on an airplane are slanted, too. As the propeller spins, it cuts into the air. The air is pushed back. This backward movement of air makes the airplane move forward. This forward motion is called thrust. Some airplanes have two or more propellers. More propellers develop more thrust.

ACTIVITY

You can make a propeller cart. It will show you how thrust moves an airplane forward to help overcome gravity. For this activity you will need:

A heavy elastic band	A toy propeller
Four toy wheels	2 pieces of wood (1 x 3 inches)
4 nails	A piece of wood (3 x 5 inches)

Nail the wheels to the piece of wood (3 x 5 inches) as shown in the drawing on the next page. Allow them to turn easily.

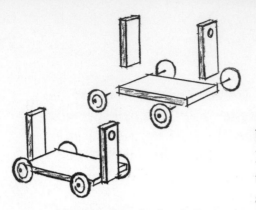

Nail the two pieces of wood (1 x 3 inches) to each end of the base as shown in the drawing. Drill a small hole through one of the uprights. The hole should be about one-half inch from the top.

Insert the shaft of the toy propeller through the hole. Attach the rubber band to the propeller shaft and to the other upright. Wind the propeller. Place the cart on a smooth surface. The propeller will develop enough thrust to move the cart forward, but not enough to lift it off the ground.

HELICOPTERS AND GRAVITY

A helicopter does not have any wings. Horizontal propellers, or rotors, lift it into the air. The rotor can be tilted to move the helicopter forward or backwards or sideways. Maybe you have also seen a helicopter remain practically motionless in the air.

This kind of air flight was one of the earliest methods of flight to be considered. Leonardo da Vinci was interested in its possibilities. Sir George Cayley's "aerial carriage" was a model design using revolving discs.

Sir George Cayley's
"aerial carriage"

When a helicopter rises, the air pushes downward. The downward push overcomes gravity and makes the helicopter rise. Air pressure is at work again.

Could you explain why a helicopter would not work in a vacuum where there is no air pressure?

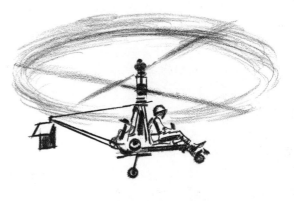

This one-man helicopter can travel about 52 miles an hour. It can rise to an altitude of a mile. The advantage of a helicopter is that it can land and take off in a very small area. It can reach places that an airplane cannot. Helicopters are used for rescues at sea, in fighting fires, for traffic control, for hauling construction equipment into rugged terrain.

The YHC-1B, a giant helicopter designed for use by the U. S. Army, can carry 33 passengers. It weighs 33,000 pounds and can travel 175 miles an hour. The earth's gravitational pull on the craft is overcome by the two rotors.

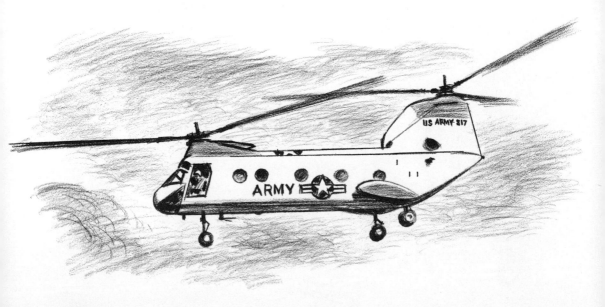

FALLING BODIES

If you ever jumped off a diving board you became a falling body. The spring of the diving board gave you an upward lift. You remained motionless for a fraction of a second at the peak of the jump. After that, you fell towards the earth's center.

There is a new sport that depends on gravity. It is called sky diving. The participant jumps out of an airplane and does not open his parachute immediately. The "fun" of the sport is to free fall as long as you dare. This sport is not one recommended for weaklings.

One of the longest falls on record was made for the U. S. Air Force by Captain Joseph W. Kittinger, Jr. He jumped from an open balloon gondola at a height of 102,800 feet and fell for 16 miles before his main parachute opened. His free fall lasted 4½ minutes and he traveled at up to 614 miles per hour.

But falling bodies are not just human bodies. They can be any object, such as a leaf, a piece of paper, a stone. For a long time early scientists thought that heavier objects fell faster than light ones. It was not too difficult for them to come to this conclusion, for they had seen an acorn fall faster than a leaf.

Galileo Galilei, who lived in the sixteenth century, was a scientist who believed that all objects fell at the same rate of speed. There is a story told that Galileo performed an experiment from the Leaning Tower in Pisa, Italy. He climbed the stairs to the top of the tower and dropped two balls of different weights at the same time. A crowd had gathered to see the experiment, because until this time people believed that different weights fell at different speeds. The two balls struck the ground at the same time. Many people who saw the objects hit the ground at the same time refused to believe what they saw.

ACTIVITY

You can perform an experiment like the one Galileo did from the Tower. You will not need to climb a tower. A chair will do just as well. You will need a ball bearing and a marble the same size. (The steel bearing is heavier.) Now stand on a chair. (Be careful, don't become a falling body.) Drop the two balls to the floor at the same time. The balls will strike the floor at the same instant.

A falling leaf does not fall as fast as an acorn because air offers more resistance to the leaf. A leaf has a greater surface area than an acorn for the air to press upward. If both were placed in a vacuum, they would fall at the same rate of speed since there would be no air resistance to slow down the object with the greater surface area.

A parachute is a freely falling body that takes advantage of air resistance. It does not fall as fast as a bomb dropped from an airplane. Do you know why? Can you explain why a parachute would not work in a vacuum?

Many objects from outer space fall to the earth. They come close enough to our planet to be attracted to it by its gravitational pull. Millions of meteorites fall to earth daily at very high speeds. Meteorites are parts of meteors, and some scientists believe that meteors come from the tails of comets. Most meteors burn up to fine dust when they enter the earth's atmosphere because of the frictional heat produced when they rub against the molecules of air.

Objects gain speed as they fall. Galileo found that a freely falling body increases its speed at the rate of 32 feet per second. At the end of one second a falling object has covered a distance of 16 feet, but at the end of that first second it is traveling at a speed of 32 feet per second. An object that has fallen for two seconds reaches a speed of 64 feet per second. At the end of the third second the object is now traveling 96 feet per second. By adding 32 feet for each second, you can determine the speed of a freely falling object.

It takes a very long time for a meteorite to fall to the earth. Can you imagine how fast a large meteorite is traveling when it hits the earth?

You can prove that a freely falling body increases its speed as it falls. You will need a marble and some clay for this activity. Flatten the clay and place it on the floor. Hold the marble about six inches over the clay. Drop the marble. Examine the impression made in the clay.

Now hold the marble about six feet above the clay and drop it. Compare the impressions made in the clay. Which made the deeper impression? Why?

Did you ever throw a ball straight into the air and wonder how high it went? It is not too difficult for you to find out. When a ball is thrown into the air, the earth's gravitational pull soon slows it down. It reaches a certain height and then falls to earth. It behaves like a freely falling body from the highest point to the time it strikes the ground.

It takes the same amount of time for the ball to go up as it does to come down.

The gravitational pull of the earth causes any object to fall with an acceleration of about 32 feet per second per second. (This means that for each second it falls it increases its speed at the rate of 32 feet per second.) The pull of gravity also decelerates — slows down — objects thrown into the air at the rate of 32 feet per second per second.

If a ball is in the air five seconds, you can find out how high it traveled by using this formula:

Distance = ½ x g x time x time

(g equals 32 feet per second per second)

Since it takes the same time for the ball to go up as it does to come down, the time it takes the ball to fall from the highest point is 2½ seconds. Therefore:

Distance = ½ x 32 x 2½ x 2½   or

Distance = 100 feet

The velocity or speed of the ball when it hit the ground can be found by using this formula:

Velocity = g x time   Therefore:

Velocity = 32 x 2½   or

Velocity = 80 feet per second

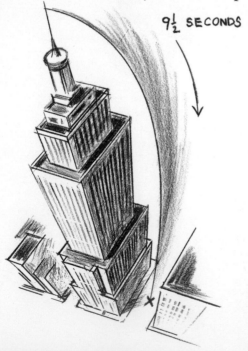

9½ SECONDS

The Empire State Building in New York City is 1,472 feet high, counting the height of the antenna.

If an object were dropped from the top of the antenna, it would take about 9½ seconds for it to reach the ground, neglecting any air resistance.

It would be traveling 304 feet per second, or about 207 miles an hour when it struck the pavement.

One of the most fascinating acts in a circus is the tightrope walker. Do you know why it is possible for him to walk on a tightrope or wire? It is gravity at work again. The performer balances himself so that his center of gravity is directly over the wire.

The center of gravity is the point in an object at which all the weight of that object seems to be concentrated. As long as the tightrope walker keeps his weight concentrated over the wire, he is balanced. If his weight should shift to one side, his center of gravity is no longer directly over the rope. He would be off balance, and would be pulled to the ground by gravity.

Many tightrope walkers hold a long pole below their waistline. The pole lowers the center of gravity and makes it easier for them to balance themselves.

ACTIVITY

Balance one end of a yardstick on a finger. Notice how you must move your finger to keep the yardstick balanced. Each time you move your finger you are changing the center of gravity so that it is over your finger. As long as the center of gravity is over your finger, the yardstick remains balanced.

It is not too difficult to balance a ruler. It is straight and regularly shaped. However, an object that has an irregular shape, such as the stone in the drawing, proposes a more difficult problem.

There is a point where the stone will balance. If this point were found, it would be possible to balance the stone on the sharp point of a pencil. It would be a strange sight to see.

ACTIVITY

You can find the center of gravity of an irregular object such as a flat piece of cardboard. For this experiment, you will need:

A piece of cardboard
Wooden stand and nail
String
A weight

Cut the piece of cardboard in an irregular shape similar to the one shown in the drawing. Punch two holes in the cardboard as shown in the drawing. (The two holes can be at any points.) Hammer a nail near the top of the wooden stand.

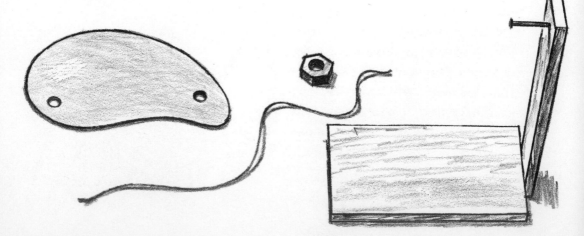

Hang the piece of cardboard to the nail in the wooden stand from one of the punched holes. Tie the weight to the string. Now suspend the string and weight to the nail. Draw a line on the cardboard by marking along the length of the string as it supports the weight.

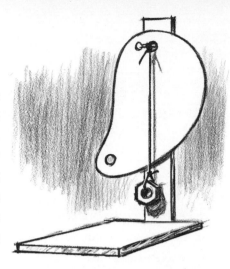

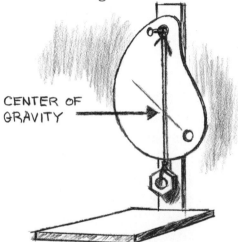

CENTER OF GRAVITY →

The weight hanging vertically is being attracted to the center of the earth by the pull of gravity. Now remove the cardboard and hang it from the other hole. Draw another line on the cardboard so that it follows the length of the string supporting the weight in this position. The two lines will intersect. The point where they cross is the center of gravity for this object.

See if you can balance the piece of cardboard on a sharp object, such as a pencil point. Don't get discouraged if you cannot do it. It is very difficult to balance irregularly shaped objects, even after you have found the center of gravity.

The gravitational pull of the earth acts on all objects, regular or irregular. In a round, solid ball the center of gravity is the center of the ball. In an irregularly shaped object, such as the cardboard in this activity, it could be at any point, depending on the shape of the object.

The Leaning Tower of Pisa is famous for many reasons. It is the place where Galileo is said to have performed the experiment to prove that objects of different weights fall at the same rate of speed. But the Tower is also famous because it has been leaning since the time it was erected. It leans about 14 feet to one side. People are amazed that the Leaning Tower does not fall over.

ACTIVITY

You can discover why the Leaning Tower of Pisa does not fall over by making a model of your own.

Cut the Tower out of a heavy piece of cardboard. Make it four inches wide and 12 inches high, as shown in the drawing.

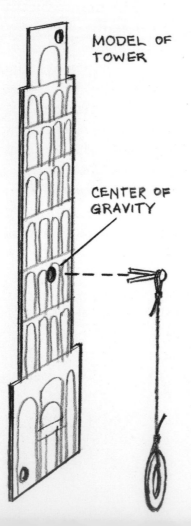

MODEL OF TOWER

CENTER OF GRAVITY

Punch two holes in your Tower model and find its center of gravity as you did in the last activity.

After you have found the center of gravity of the Tower, punch a hole at this point. Insert a paper fastener in the hole. Tie one end of a piece of string to the fastener. Tie a nut (a weight) to the other end of the string.

Then take another piece of heavy cardboard that is bigger than your Tower model. Fold up one end of this piece of cardboard to make a ledge at the bottom. (Or fasten a strip of wood at the bottom to make the ledge for the Tower to rest on.)

LEDGE →

Hold the cardboard with the ledge in an upright position. Place your model on the ledge so that its base sits on the ledge.

Then, tilt the cardboard so that the weight hanging from the string on the model does not fall outside the base of the Tower. The Tower will lean, but it will not fall over because its center of gravity is still within the base.

Now tilt the cardboard so that the weight does fall outside the Tower's base. When the Tower is in this position, the center of gravity falls outside the base of the Tower. The Tower will topple over because the center of gravity is outside its base. The Leaning Tower of Pisa does not lean enough to have this happen.

An automobile, like any other object, has a center of gravity. Some automobiles are taller and heavier than others. The center of gravity in a loaded truck is higher than in a low-built sports car.

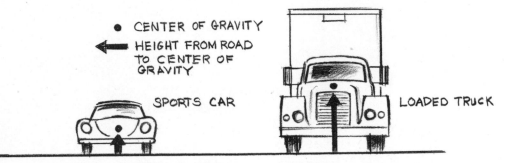

Have you ever noticed how you lean to one side in a car when it is traveling around a curve? If a car travels too fast around a curve, it can turn over. When a car leans too much, the center of gravity falls outside the base of the car. This causes the car to turn over.

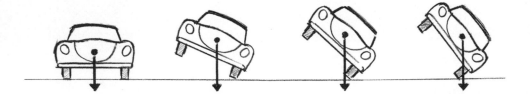

Racing cars have very low centers of gravity. They can travel around curves much faster than regular cars without fear of turning over.

Cut out a sports car and a big truck from cardboard. The sports car will be lower built than the truck. Make them both four inches wide. Find the center of gravity for each one as you did for the irregularly shaped piece of cardboard and for the Tower model. Punch a hole at this point. Insert a paper fastener in the hole. Tie one end of a piece of string to the paper fastener. Tie a weight to the other end of the string.

Place the truck on the big piece of cardboard with the ledge on it that you used in the Tower activity.

See how far you can tilt the truck before it turns over.

COMPARE DIFFERENCES IN TILT

Now place the sports car on the cardboard. See how far you can tilt it before it turns over. Is it more or less than the big truck? Why?

THE PENDULUM

Galileo Galilei was only nineteen years old when he made a startling discovery in a cathedral in Pisa, Italy. One evening in the year 1583, while attending the services, he noticed a lamp that was suspended from the ceiling by a long chain. It was swaying back and forth. Perhaps someone had given it a slight push. As Galileo watched it for a long period of time he noted that the lamp seemed to take the same amount of time to complete each swing. Since he did not have a watch to time the swings, he used his pulse beat instead.

After he left the cathedral, Galileo went home and began to experiment with pendulums of different weights and lengths. He discovered that successive swings of a pendulum took the same time when the arc was small.

He also found out through experiments that the weight of the pendulum did not affect the time of its swing.

Did you ever swing together with a friend? Did you ever try swinging in separate swings but side by side? You may have noticed that even though your friend weighed more or less than you, he did not swing any faster.

You can prove that the weight of a pendulum does not affect the time of its swing. For this experiment you will need two pendulums exactly the same length. Cut two pieces of cord three feet long. Attach an eraser to the end of one piece of cord. Attach three erasers to the end of the other piece of cord.

Suspend both pendulums from the top of a doorway. Make sure that they are both the same length. Now swing both pendulums at the same time with an equal amount of force. They will both swing back and forth the same distance. The heavier pendulum does not swing faster.

Many years later Galileo suggested to his son, Vincenzio, that a pendulum might be used to keep time. Many men besides Vincenzio Galilei experimented with pendulum clocks during the sixteenth century. But it was Christian Huygens who is considered the inventor of the pendulum clock.

Many kinds of pendulum clocks are still in use all over the world. The back and forth motion of the pendulum turns the gears and moves the hands of the clock. A grandfather's clock that stands on the floor is a pendulum clock.

ACTIVITY

Tie one end of a piece of cord about 46 inches long to an eraser. Measure off 39 inches on the length of cord. Suspend the 39-inch long pendulum from the top of a doorway, using either a tack or masking tape. Push the pendulum so that it swings freely. Use a watch with a second hand to determine how long it takes for the pendulum to swing back and forth.

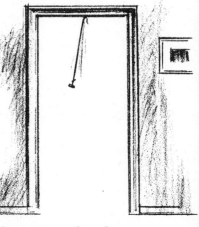

It will take approximately one second to swing from one side to the other.

Now make a pendulum 78 inches long. Suspend it from the top of a doorway. Give the pendulum a push as you did the shorter one. How long does it take to swing from one side to the other?

You have probably discovered that a pendulum will not take exactly twice as long to swing from one side to the other just because its length is exactly twice as long.

A pendulum would have to be 156 inches long before it would take two seconds to swing from one side to the other.

A plumb line is a pendulum that has stopped swinging. It is really a weight suspended on a cord or chain. It is used to find a vertical line at any point. Gravity attracts the weight to the center of the earth, making the weight hang vertically.

Sometimes a plumb line does not point exactly to the center of the earth. The rocks and soil in the ground do not weigh the same in all parts of the world. A plumb line can be attracted to an area nearby that has more weight under its surface.

The plumb line in the drawing is slanted to the left because it is being attracted by the heavier materials in the ground in area A.

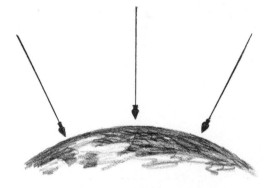

A

A surveyor uses a plumb line to help him find property boundary lines. His transit is set over a corner marker. A plumb line is hung from the transit. The transit is moved until the pointed end of the plumb bob (weight) points at the corner marker. Sometimes a corner marker consists of a piece of wood with a nail driven into it. The nail serves as the point where the two sides of a piece of property meet.

Some builders use a plumb line to be certain that the walls of a building are going up straight. Imagine a building as long as the distance from New York to San Francisco. If a plumb line were used to set up the vertical walls, the sides of the building would look like this:

The sides of this building would not be parallel. If the lines were extended long enough, they would meet at the center of the earth. Parallel lines do not meet.

The base of a large building can be several hundred feet square. Its sides would appear parallel because the building covers a very small part of the earth's curved surface.

The early Romans used a large slingshot to hurl stones at their enemy. This was one of the first missile launchers. It was called a *ballista*. The word ballistics is derived from this word.

The path of a bullet or projectile is determined by its speed, or velocity, and by gravity. A bullet in flight is constantly being pulled to the earth by the force of gravity. The force of gravity and the velocity of the projectile act independently.

You can demonstrate the effects of velocity and gravity. Hold two pencils in your right hand as shown in the drawing.

Strike the end of one of the pencils with a finger of your other hand so that it shoots out. At the same instant, drop your right hand quickly so that the other pencil falls.

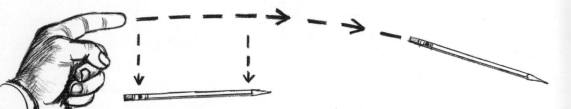

The pencils will hit the floor at the same time. Repeat the experiment. This time strike the one pencil harder so that it travels a greater distance.

Both pencils will still reach the floor at the same time. The pencil that you flicked with your finger behaved like a bullet in flight. Once a bullet leaves the barrel of a gun, it becomes a freely falling body and falls at the rate of 32 feet per second. This rate will be slightly less if there is air resistance. However, the law of gravity holds whether an object is falling vertically or moving forward as it falls.

16 FEET

ONE SECOND

A freely falling body will fall 16 feet in the first second. If a gun is fired horizontally from a height of 16 feet, the bullet will hit the ground in one second. A ball dropped from a height of 16 feet the instant the gun is fired will reach the ground at the same time the bullet does.

MORE THAN 16 FEET

If the gun is raised, the bullet will travel a greater distance. It will go up for a brief while and then down.

A gun that is elevated (raised) at an angle of 45 degrees will make the bullet travel the greatest distance. If the angle is greater than 45 degrees, the bullet will travel higher but not as far. If the angle is less than 45 degrees, gravity pulls the bullet to the earth too soon to gain much distance.

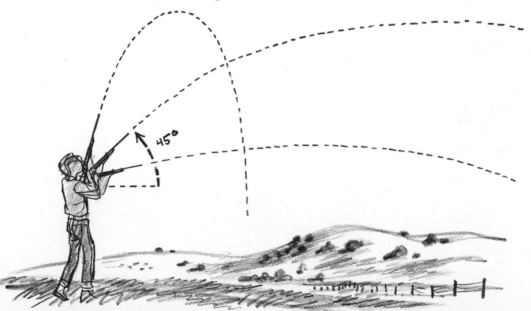

45°

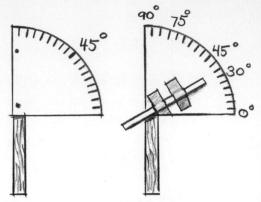

You can make a simple gadget that will show you how an object will travel the greatest distance when it is projected at an angle of 45 degrees.

Cut out a quarter circle from a heavy piece of cardboard. Nail it to a stick as shown in the drawing. Using a protractor, mark off the quarter circle at 5 degree intervals. Using masking tape, attach a straw to the quarter circle as shown in the drawing. Set the straw at an angle of 30 degrees.

Now hold the gadget on a table top so that the stick is perpendicular to the top of the table. Insert a dried pea into the straw, and blow. Have a friend mark the point where the dried pea hit the table or floor.

Angle the straw at 75 degrees. Insert another dried pea into the straw. Blow into the straw again. Have your friend mark the point where the second pea lands.

Now move the straw to the 45 degree marking. Blow into the straw with a pea in it again. You will observe that the dried pea traveled the greatest distance when the straw was set at the 45 degree angle.

44

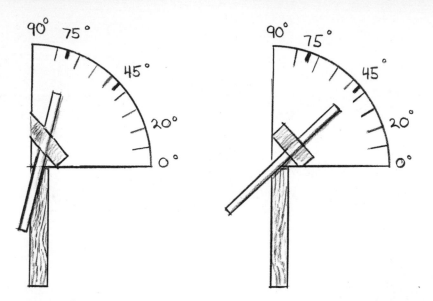

Target shooting can be fun when you hit the target. If you aim directly at a target a considerable distance away, the bullet will land below it. How much below depends upon your distance from the target and the speed of the bullet. But the rear sight on a rifle can be adjusted to compensate for the pull of gravity on the bullet in flight.

Adjusting the rear sight of the rifle raises the barrel slightly, as shown in the drawing.

Large warships shoot shells many miles at enemy ships. Sometimes the large guns are elevated very high. Can you explain why? Practically all of the calculations to determine the angle of elevation are done electronically. There are many things that must be known before the exact elevation of the large guns is set. The distance to the target, the speed of both ships, and even the rotation of the earth must be considered to determine the correct angle of elevation.

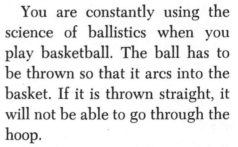

You are constantly using the science of ballistics when you play basketball. The ball has to be thrown so that it arcs into the basket. If it is thrown straight, it will not be able to go through the hoop.

It takes practice to make a basket, but a knowledge of simple ballistics helps. Remember that the amount of arc depends upon the speed at which you throw the ball and on gravity.

There are other sports in which a knowledge of ballistics helps you to be a better player. A baseball player uses ballistics, too. If an outfielder attempted to throw the ball level with the ground, it would not travel far.

Instead, he arcs the ball high into the air. By doing this, it takes gravity a longer time to pull the ball to the ground. In the meantime, the ball will travel a greater distance.

A bomb dropped from an airplane will not travel straight down. It will travel in a curved path.

The bombardier releases the bomb quite a distance from the target. How far away he releases the bomb depends upon the speed and altitude of the airplane. Wind direction and speed must be considered, too.

During the war, fighter planes used tracer bullets in the machine guns to "zero in" on an enemy plane. A tracer bullet has a small firework attached to mark its flight by a trail of smoke or fire. The pilots could actually see the bullets travel to the target. They knew that the bullets started to drop as soon as they left the barrels of the machine guns.

The sights on the machine guns were adjusted to take into account the pull of gravity on the bullets. The gunners also shot ahead of the enemy plane because it took time for the bullets to reach the target.

If they aimed directly at the enemy airplane, it would not be in that same place when the bullets got there.

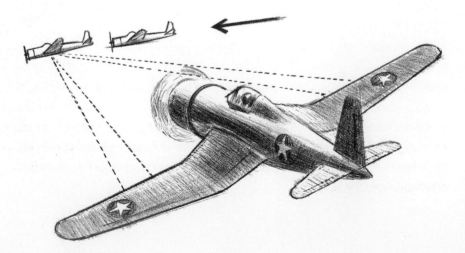

THE MOON AND THE TIDES

The earth's diameter is about four times larger than the moon's diameter. Since the moon is smaller than the earth, its gravitational pull is less.

Sports events on the moon would be great fun. Sports would take on a new look because of the lesser pull of gravity. The record for the high jump on earth is over seven feet. The same high jumper on the moon would be able to clear 42 feet. Broad jumpers would be able to clear a football field in two leaps. A champion javelin thrower would be able to hurl his pointed spear about a quarter of a mile.

The tides have fascinated people for many centuries. Thousands of years ago people believed that the moon caused the tides in some strange way, but they did not know how or what caused the waters to rise and fall.

All bodies in the universe attract each other. The earth is pulling on the moon. The gravitational pull of the earth holds the moon in orbit. The moon also pulls on the earth.

The gravitational pull of the moon causes the land on the earth to rise about a half foot and the atmosphere that blankets the earth to expand several miles. But most important of all, the moon's gravitational pull causes the water on the earth to rise and fall.

The sun helps to cause the tides, too. It is much larger than the moon, but because it is so far away from the earth its effect on the waters of the earth is not as great as the moon's. However, there are times when the moon and the sun are in a line so that the combined pulls of the moon and the sun cause higher tides.

This happens twice a month when the moon is new and full. The tides during this time have a special name. They are called "spring tides." This name is given to the tides because the combined gravitational pulls of the moon and the sun make the water "spring" out.

The gravitational pulls of the moon and the sun tend to oppose each other when they are at right angles. The tides during this time are not too high. They are called "neap tides" from an Old English word that means "low." Neap tides occur during the first and third quarters of the moon.

All bodies of water feel the influence of these gravitational pulls. Lakes and rivers have tides, although in most of them the difference between high and low tide is not noticeable.

Since all bodies in the universe have an attraction for each other, even the artificial satellites that circle the earth have a pull of gravity. They pull on the waters of the world just like the moon and sun. They even pull on the water in your bathtub. So does the sun and moon. But you will not be able to detect high and low tide in your bathtub. The amount of gravitational pull would be far too little to be seen.

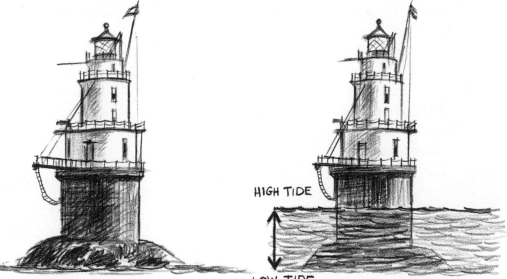

HIGH TIDE

LOW TIDE

Tides are not the same in all places. Some waters rise as little as two feet, but in the Bay of Fundy, off Nova Scotia, high tide may be as much as 50 feet. Tide tables for major seaports are calculated for the use of ships.

There is no water on the moon, but you can imagine the kind of tides there would be on the moon if it was covered by oceans. The tides on the moon would be higher than the tides on earth. Can you explain why? Remember that the gravitational pull of the earth is much greater than that of the moon.

SPACE CAPSULES

Yuri Gagarin, the Russian cosmonaut, was the first man to orbit the earth in a spacecraft. In 1962, John Glenn became the first American to orbit the globe. But without the help of gravity none of the astronauts could have made their orbital trips.

Have you ever seen a football player throw a long pass? Did you notice how the ball traveled in a curved path to the receiver's arms? Gravity was pulling the football to the earth as it traveled through the air.

Imagine a football player about 100 miles above the earth. Suppose he could throw a football at a speed of 17,000 miles an hour. The speed of the ball would offset the pull of gravity on the ball. It would appear to be falling towards the earth but would never get there. Instead, it would orbit the earth for some time.

17,000 MILES AN HOUR

Space capsules behave in the same way. The speed of a capsule in orbit is called "orbital velocity." The inward pull of gravity on the capsule must be balanced by this velocity in order to have the space capsule remain in orbit. Since gravity decreases with distance, so does orbital velocity.

At a point C in space, the velocity of the satellite does not have to be as fast as the velocity at A or B. Satellites do not all follow the same orbits. Some have larger orbits than others. The orbit of a satellite depends upon its speed and its distance from the earth.

The moon travels more slowly than artificial satellites or space capsules because it is a greater distance from the earth. The artificial satellites must travel much faster than the moon to stay in orbit because of the greater pull of gravity closer to the earth. The moon is about 240,000 miles away from the earth. It travels about one-half mile a second. An artificial satellite at an altitude of 200 miles must travel about 4½ miles per second to remain in orbit.

ACTIVITY

Here is an activity that will show you that the closer an object is to the earth, the faster it must travel to remain in orbit. You will need: two pieces of cord (1 foot and 5 feet) and some clay.

Make two balls of clay the same size. Tie a ball of clay to one end of the 1-foot length of cord. Tie the other ball of clay to one end of the 5-foot cord.

Swing the clay ball on the 5-foot cord over your head. Notice how fast it must travel to remain "in orbit." Now swing the other clay ball at the same speed. It will not revolve because that speed is too slow. In order for the clay ball on the 1-foot cord to "stay in orbit," you must swing it faster than the ball on the longer cord.

ORBITS AND GRAVITY

The scientist must control the speed, direction and the elevation of a satellite for it to be fixed in a stable orbit. If the orbital velocity attained is exactly right to precisely balance the outward pull—centrifugal force—against the inward pull—gravity—then the satellite will follow a circular path around the earth.

But if the satellite's velocity is excessive for its altitude, then the man-made moon will follow an elliptical orbit. Gravity and centrifugal force are not exactly in balance.

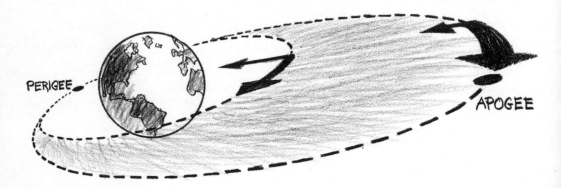

It will move outwards and lose speed at the point farthest from the earth (apogee) and will move with increased speed to the point nearest the earth where it began its orbital flight (perigee).

ESCAPING EARTH'S GRAVITY

The apogee will move farther out into space as the velocity of the satellite increases. If the satellite is traveling fast enough, it may break away from an elliptical orbit around the earth. This is called "escape velocity." The escape velocity at the earth's surface is equal to 25,000 miles an hour. At this speed, the satellite would have no apogee and no orbit. It would shoot out into space and never return.

A rocket carrying a space capsule does not have to travel 25,000 miles an hour to escape the earth's gravitational pull. If it could continue traveling straight up at a speed of 10 miles an hour, it would eventually reach an altitude where gravity is practically zero. However, to escape the earth's gravity at a speed of 10 miles an hour would not be practical. It would require thousands of tons of fuel to lift a fraction of a pound.

LIFE EXPECTANCY OF SATELLITES

Artificial satellites travel in air that is much thinner than the air found at sea level. Even though the air is very thin, it still produces a certain amount of drag that decreases the speed of the satellite.

As the satellite gets closer to the earth, gravity overbalances its velocity. It loses orbital speed and altitude. Soon it comes into contact with the denser part of the atmosphere where it disintegrates due to frictional heat.

Heat is energy in motion. Frictional heat is caused by the bombardment of air molecules against the satellite.

ACTIVITY

Fill a pan with cold water. Put your hand in the water. You do not feel any heat because the water molecules are not moving rapidly.

Empty the pan. Fill it with warm water. You can now feel the heat because the water molecules are moving faster against your hand.

SPACE STATIONS

Many scientists visualize the shape of a space station as a huge doughnut. If a space station could be located somewhere above our atmosphere, it could be used as a refueling station for the space ships going to the moon.

The space station would travel in orbit at a speed of about 18,000 miles an hour. The construction of the space station would be done in free orbit. Weightlessness in space would make construction jobs easy. Tons of material could be lifted by one hand. Wires would be used instead of girders since there would be no stresses on structures in free orbit. The members of space construction crews would travel in free orbit with the materials that were shot up into space by rockets. The men would simply collect the parts and assemble them. They would be traveling 18,000 miles an hour while they are assembling the parts to the space station. But they would not be aware of any motion since everything would be moving with them at the same speed in free orbit.

There is no gravity in free orbit to pull things down. In fact, there is no up or down in space. The men working on the space station would not be aware of any up or down. Someone would appear "up" only if he were over one's head.

Both men in the drawing think that the other is "up."

Moving in space in a weightless condition will not be an easy thing to do. The members of the construction crews will probably have to take extensive training to learn how to move about in space. A fast movement of the body would send a person spinning out of control.

Jet guns will help man move about in space. The jet gun works on the jet propulsion principle. The rush of air out of the nozzle of the gun pushes the gun and the spaceman in the opposite direction. It is the same principle that is used to send rockets into space.

An inflated balloon reacts in the same way when it is released and the air allowed to escape from the opening.

Maybe the foreman on a construction job in outer space will travel about in a small jet car. He will be able to control the direction of the small craft by moving the jet nozzles on the sides of the jet car.

The flying belt might be another way people will move about in space where there is a lack of gravity. A large flying belt has already been invented and tested. Some day it may be miniaturized and used in outer space by the members of the construction crews. Time will tell.

PROBLEMS OF WEIGHTLESSNESS

Without gravity in space, there may be many problems that will confront the space traveler. Cooking, earth style, would be very difficult. If someone attempted to flip pancakes, the pancakes would flip around the room with the cook doing flips along with them.

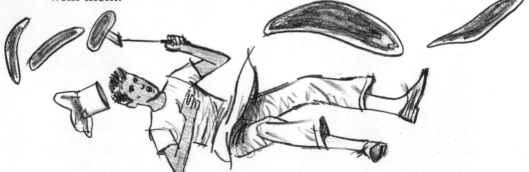

Drinking water from a glass becomes a problem, too. Water stays in a glass because of gravity. Without gravity, the water would tend to form droplets that would spill out into the room. Countless water droplets would drift about the room.

Plastic bottles will replace drinking glasses in situations where there is no gravity. By squeezing the plastic bottle, the water is forced into the mouth by the pressure inside the bottle.

If you think that washing dishes on earth is a problem, wait until you try to do them when there is no gravity. Gravity holds the water in the kitchen sink. Without gravity, dishes, cups and other eating utensils would drift around the room.

If you decided that life inside the space station was too hectic, a "siesta" outside the space station would help calm your nerves. Since there is no sound in space, there would be no noises to bother you. Without gravity, one would drift in free orbit, enjoying the peacefulness of space. Of course, you would have a line attached to the station so that you wouldn't wake up and find that you had drifted off into outer space.

ARTIFICIAL GRAVITY

The problems of weightlessness due to lack of gravity in a space station can be solved by producing artificial gravity. This can be done by rotating the space stations once every seven seconds. The action of the spinning space station would produce a force that would be the same as gravity.

Maybe you have seen a motorcyclist ride on a curved wall at the circus. The cyclist does not fall because he is going fast enough for centrifugal force to overcome the pull of gravity towards the center of the track.

ACTIVITY

Ordinarily, water in a pail will fall out when you turn it upside down, because of gravity. You can produce artificial gravity in the pail, and the water will not fall out.

Fill a pail about half full of water, and swing it in a circular motion as shown in the drawing. The force you feel, pulling outward, holds the water in the pail.

At all points in the space station, "up" would be towards the center. Men on the opposite sides of the space station would be standing with their heads towards each other. The artificial gravity would decrease as the men walked towards the center of the space station.

There would be no artificial gravity at the central axis of the space station. A person would be weightless when he was at the center of the station.

Designers of the space station will probably find that it will be more economical to stack space stations on top of each other to revolve on the same axis. Gravity would be produced artificially at all levels.

The multi-level space station will look like a stack of doughnuts. The people in the space stations will be able to use elevators to get to the various levels.

Life in the space station will be more enjoyable with the problems of weightlessness solved by using artificial gravity. However, the help in the kitchen must remember not to throw the garbage out of the space station. Any object that is thrown from a space station will attain the same speed as the station. Chicken bones, empty cans and soda bottles would become artificial satellites traveling in the same orbit with the space station. For this reason, any garbage will be placed in containers and brought back to earth.

GRAVITY ON OTHER PLANETS

There are nine known planets in our solar system. The sun is the center of the solar system. It is about 93 million miles away from the earth. Look at the drawing. Which planet is closest to the sun? Which planet is the greatest distance from the sun? The planets travel around the sun at different speeds. They are kept in orbit by two forces: the sun's gravity and centrifugal force.

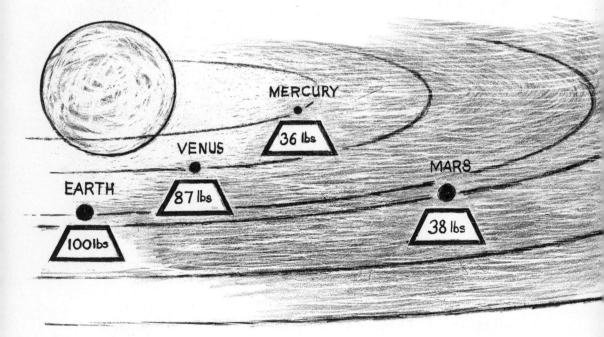

The sun pulls on all the planets. The planets that are closer to the sun must travel faster than the more distant planets to stay in orbit. Mercury, the closest planet to the sun, travels about 30 miles a second. Pluto, the farthest away, travels about 3 miles a second.

Each planet has a gravitational pull of its own. The gravitational pulls of the planets are not the same because they are of different weights.

You would not be the same weight on the various planets as you are on earth. But you do not have to go to the other planets to find out what you would weigh on each one. There are scales at the American Museum of Natural History in New York City that will register your weight as it would be on the other planets.

Pluto is too far away for its exact gravitational pull—and thus its weight—to be known yet. But see what would happen to a 100-pound person on Mars or Jupiter.

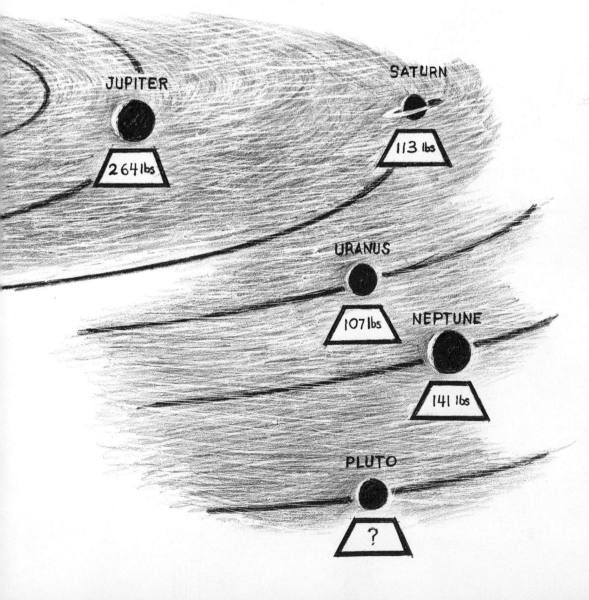

JUPITER

264 lbs

SATURN

113 lbs

URANUS

107 lbs

NEPTUNE

141 lbs

PLUTO

?

INDEX